WOMAN : PLANT : LANGUAGE

Agata Masłowska was born in Poland and lives in Scotland. Her poetry and fiction have appeared in various magazines and journals. She is the recipient of the Scottish Book Trust Award and the Hawthornden Writing Fellowship.

Woman: Plant: Language

AGATA MASŁOWSKA

BAD BETTY PRESS

First published in 2025 by Bad Betty Press
Cobden Place, Cobden Chambers, Nottingham NG1 2ED

badbettypress.com

PB ISBN: 978-1-913268-76-3
EPUB ISBN: 978-1-913268-77-0

A CIP record of this book is available from the British Library.

Cover art: 'hear their thoughts distilled :: crocuses & pansies' (wet botanical ink print) © Elżbieta Wójcik-Leese
Interior images ©Agata Masłowska
Source text p61-64 ©Anna Tsing

Book design by Amy Acre

Printed and bound in the UK by TJ Books, Padstow, Cornwall using FSC® Certified paper from responsibly managed forests

It was a larch tree. It is the only tree I can identify, with certainty. (...) The sea-green needles are like silk and speckled, it always seemed to me, with little red, how shall I say, with little red specks.

—Samuel Beckett, *Molloy*

A nomadic poetics will cross languages, not just translate, but write in all or any of them. (...) We will write in foreign languages (real or made-up ones) in order to come to the realization that all languages are foreign.

—Pierre Joris, *A Nomad Poetics*

CONTENTS

Woman : Plant : Language

LEMON

Once we were talking
about our death
as if it belonged elsewhere

You cut the lemon half-way
it tasted sour, it still does
but death seems closer

Okay, look at the tree outside
the way it bends in the wind under the sterile sky
trees seem eternal, unlike lemons

I count my inhalations
one two
three

I'm talking to you as if
you are or were alive
four

Time five plays its game
against us
six

I'm no longer talking
seven
I'm writing things down

To remember
eight
nine

This obsession with dying
ten
when I can still

Nine
lemons are different from tomatoes
despite their roundness

A pen and a straw are lines
eight
I'm not trying to play things down

I loved you, when love wasn't given a time slot,
when touch
seven

Now I love you far
let's get in virtual touch
six

Did you hear about the animal which
five
no never mind

Yes this is just a surface
today I'm breathing here
four I could tell you about

And go deeper – I know –
would be better
three

All the stories of flora
two
that would make you

But what's more important
now than

FEMALE FIGS CLOSED ON ALL SIDES, SUPPOSED TO BE MONSTERS

An inverted flower chooses to bloom for itself,
away from the sun and the moon.
A female fig keeps its ovaries in confinement.
It lets a female wasp in through an ostiole to pollinate
its inner florets. The wasp dies in a tight space,
unable to lay eggs. The fig digests it. Perhaps
it is out of mercy. If it was a male fig,
the wasp would lay the eggs and collect pollen
from male flowers on her way out. She sacrifices
her life in the end so the male fig merely postpones
the wasp's death for its own benefit.
Women often carry wasps in their chests
who hum when their cervices are examined.
If the wasp lays the eggs and fails to implant pollen
inside the fig, the tree aborts the fruit. In villages
women slaughter cows if they don't produce milk.

WOMAN DREAMS OF ESCAPE

After Joan Miró's painting by the same name

Something crashes somewhere,
inaudible here, impossible to translate

Once a young man sat next to me on a park bench

it keeps breaking, somewhere,
someone we don't know evaluates the damage

'What are you reading?'

the river flows broken sideways,
someone loses their adjectives and verbs

'Clarice Lispector,' I said.

some body forgets itself in a dream,
the roof of the house turns upwards

'I wish all women left their abusers,

rocked between the sun and the moon,
she applies blue on her eyelids there there

he said 'everyone feels their collective pain'.

HANIA AT THE END OF THE WORLD

She howls in pain, shaking her
fist at the god she hopes exists.
It's nearly time to die. Skin flaking
on the floor.

Outside the passing cars hum
like tanks, her body still remembers hiding
as a five-year-old in a potato field
dirt in her mouth, bullets overhead,
her mother's body stacked on top of hers.

First Hitler didn't kill me,
then Stalin didn't,
now I'm afraid
to put the kettle on.

At night she doesn't sleep,
rubbing remedies onto crooked fingers,
wanting to grasp at something solid,
like crochet tablecloths or baked red bricks.

The neighbours' orgasms pulse
through the walls.
Chipped Jesus, still on the cross,
looks away.

Men came hoping to marry me,
I rubbed my feet in chicken shit,
tangled hay in my hair.

She unties her hair in the orchard,
the thud of apples on the ground,
we gather to collect ripe fruit.

Having grown up in the war,
I couldn't imagine having children.

We eat plums, then run to the wooden
toilet beyond the barn. Inside a pile
of newspapers and an old copy
of *War and Peace*, not to read
but to tear pages from.

In a block of flats shit can come up the pipes
at any moment. But in the village
it stayed down in the ground. When I die
I am only afraid of being eaten by worms.

A LULLABY FOR THE TIMES OF WAR

O zoria, the evening aurora hum us to sleep lyuli lyuli
we are sent out barefoot into the snow

the clouds cannot muffle the sounds of machine thunder
birds perch on leafless trees, their beaks open lightly, feathers ruffled

O zoria, the evening aurora hum us to sleep lyuli lyuli
the silent hour ends before we can fall asleep

bombs fall on us like babies' heads rolling under our beds
words frozen on phone screens, mute emojis loaded like guns

our bodies' tissue remembers this well, we still remember it
the enemy's blank refusal to translate what we have seen

our names carry the stories of our parents and great-grandparents
we will undo this black dream, burn the tar flowing from the sky

O zoria, we are sent out barefoot into the snow, lyuli lyuli
the evening aurora hum us to sleep

DEEP HOURS

mother and I crawl
through the forest

shapes of children's voices
in a burning school, soft moss

we head towards them
trees denser than dense

mother is fast, she loads the gun
and shoots, urges me on

the men behind us
respond with dark fire

a child's song bends
in the wind, I'll save it

bullets swish by
muscles hard, deep stones

mother keeps moving,
shoots with charred hands

I turn and shoot too
the depth of the forest, sonic smoke

the rustling of children's voices
ascending

silk shadows
mother and I

black guilt
black leaves

NOONWRAITHS

We wake again to remember our exclusion from ourselves:
the wedding dresses frayed,

the darkening sun. Our placentas dried up somewhere
in the desert with no sound.

Imagine our bodies swimming, reading books, not split
into pieces. Our children

will never crave our milk. If we are not possessed
by men, we are possessed.

The twisting dust at noon. We're asking you
a question. Unmarried,

against the law. Grating absence annihilates
your crops.

Searching for space. Buffering in the heat,
we can no longer die.

And does it frighten you? Be careful.
Centuries of trembling.

Look we'd like to watch the moon
and sit in silence.

FIGS WOUNDED WITH A STRAW RIPEN SOONER

The cut sweetens the tissue; saccharine laceration. Pressing a leaf against the wound won't help it heal. Some flesh is meant to keep its wounds open. Festering emotions mistaken for love, an underdone cliché. Ripening can be as raw as gaining understanding. Experience doesn't sweeten the bitterness, but turns the tongue upside down. We cut the inflorescence into crescent moons to prevent choking. Chewing produces more saliva and aids digestion.
The movement of seeds and flowers crushed in our mouths is more expressive than the movement of our bodies. Drinking juice through a straw reduces the risk of acid and sugar damage to our teeth. Biting into a ripe fig: ecstatic.

PIEKŁO KOBIET

I. *Fifteen-year-olds sit in a classroom chatting and laughing. The desks arranged in a circle. Enter a priest.*

"Quiet please! Adamczak"

"Present"

"Ciepłuch"

"Present"

"Masłowska"

"Present"

"Unfortunately. Nitkowska"

II. *The priest smooths his hair, touches the cross on his chest*

"Let us pray: Our Father in heaven: święć się imię Twoje, przyjdź Królestwo Twoje"
"Bądź wola Twoja"
"Chleba naszego"
"I odpuść nam nasze winy"
"Zbaw nas ode złego"
"Amen"

III. *The priest writes on the blackboard, uses only capital letters. Teenagers look at the blackboard, some take notes, others sit motionless.*

"Today, we will talk about why abortion is a sin"

IV. *One of the teenagers raises her hand.*

"What if a woman has been raped, Father?"

"Masłowska, of course. If a woman is raped and doesn't want to be raped, she produces anti-bodies that kill the sperm."

V. *Two teenagers enter the classroom with clipboards to do an interview with the priest for their school zine. They look the priest up and down smiling and fixing their skirts. Masłowska goes first, then Byrkiet.*

"How many buttons do you have on your robe, Father?"

"Fifty-six."

"How many socks do you have on, Father?

"Two."

"How many metres between your desk and the door, Father?"

"Four."

"How many women die every year due to the abortion ban in Poland?"

"An insignificant number."

VI. *Some insignificant numbers*

2009: 8 women
2010–11: 9
2012: 4
2013: 7
2014: 8
2015: 6
2016–2017: 9
2018: 5
2019: 4
2020: 9
2021: 7

VII. *Some names*

Anna Magda Katarzyna Sylwia
Ewa Joanna Dominika Aleksandra
Paulina Zofia Agnieszka Ilona
Beata Anna Magda Katarzyna
Olga Monika Justyna Klementyna
Jolanta Urszula Marta Sylwia
Agata Ewa Joanna
Dominika Aleksandra Paulina Zofia
Agnieszka Ilona Beata Anna
Magda Katarzyna Olga
Monika Justyna Klementyna Jolanta
Urszula Marta Sylwia
Agata Ewa Joanna Dominika
Aleksandra Paulina Zofia
Agnieszka Ilona Beata

MOTHER'S BODY

Mother's body envelopes everything:
it is the world's totality.

I look at my breasts and see mother,
tears run down her face.

She loves and loves other bodies,
but her own.

Sometimes the fear of her body's death
catches up with her.

She folds herself into
her own womb to find love.

Mother, you are not forgotten.
Mother, you are forever loved.

WAYS IN WHICH NATURE

I. Meditaris Avena

Land covered in trees. A thought turns yellow. Falls echoing. A body in foetal position. A seed resting. Outside structures. Of flora. Trees breathing in. One another. Meditating.

II. Bryophytes

The air is full of ancient verdancy. Softness on the eyes. Following one gentle curve. And another. Non-vascular ripples. Water moves over outer surfaces. Protrusions guide it into a gentle tide. Unlike other plants, bryophytes don't drink water, but put it on their skin like a moisturiser. Water moves the sperm to the eggs. Spore flow. Gametophyte joy.

III. Marchantiophyta

Either a flat, plate-like thallus or flattened leaves. Small and overlooked. Sensitive to chemicals. If you're in for a kill, use flumioxazin, quinoclamine, and sodium carbonate peroxyhydrate. If you believe it, it might cure your liver. In asexual reproduction, gemmae disks are dispersed by rainfall. One disk after another.

IV. Sphagnum

No root, nor seed, nor flower. Sphagnum stores water in its cells like a sponge. Its lowest parts are dead and decompose, while its top keeps sphagnum alive. One century passes. Another century. Sphagnum organic matter gets compressed into peat. Burning peat releases carbon dioxide into the atmosphere where it stays for lifetimes.

A WOMAN BY THE SEA

I.

Low tide   low moon tide
low moon time   slow moon time
shallow tide   shallow sea
moon time slow
low shallow sea
shall see slowly
see shoal   low blue sea
slow blue mielizna   blue miel
slow honey   shallow blue honey sea

II.

Ember wings like leaves
leaves like bird wings
salt in the mouth of a fish
sea waves echo through the woods
peacock's calls carried over the low sea
salt liquid sound waves

Who is listening enclosed in a seashell
now open to the blue wind

Old pier drying in low tide
a misty cormorant parliament
below boats gathering rain
silence ripples through seaweed
seismic sound waves

pebbles click and click
flipped over by turnstones
invisible to the eye

Who is watching enclosed in the seashell
now open to the blue sky

III.

A body walking along a country road
a woman
alone
in the countryside
the furious sky this is no space for feelings
self aware on the edge
the shimmer of the sea in the distance
thorny blackberry bushes tiny birds over yellow flowers
every sound
not turning round skin is a border to the ocean
washed-up jellyfish rippled sand
the sea on the tip of the woman's
tongue

LIGHTHOUSE MOODS

Crumbling edges where the land meets the water, where the water eats the land. The clouds have gathered low amassing all knowledge from their own reflection. The sky is floating over the water surface. The rain is coming on slow like migraine. Dip your toe in cool water before you leave. Hide tide. High time to go into the sea. The lighthouse is waiting to be launched

into space.

The sun is off and sea-birds are hiding. The horizon invites your eye to rest on it. Go through the opening and out, slow movement of the bones. The water carries you. Hazy clouds froth your head. The lighthouse, a chess tower, anticipates the sea's next move. The game might go on forever. Do not hold your breath. Underwater sea creatures go on unaffected by your breathing.

Smooth elements. Clarity is rare. The air carries the smell of fish. The lighthouse has many words for the sea. It has seen everything. Is your body as massive and unknowable as the body of water? Unlike your body the sea belongs to no one. The hills on the horizon in the shades of blue water merging into the sky. How are you transforming? Lean over and see your own reflection. Wash your face and let the salt sting your skin. Taste it with your tongue.

MOHO BISHOPI

The Bishop's ʻōʻō or Molokai ʻōʻō (Moho bishopi) was the penultimate member of the extinct genus of the ʻōʻōs (Moho) within the extinct family Mohoidae.

took-took the haunted land they took a tree and then
the next one and on and ʻōʻō my song is dim despite
the bright blue vastness of the sky how deceptive
their benign took-took I wing out shapes in honey
air leaving no trace the shimmer of my wings will echo
in their memories without a sound indifferent now
they took the land and then some more and on and on
and ʻōʻō the river knows my story it ripples through
the soil the compost polyphony of lost songs each
a different language took-took my bones will soon
fossil worshipped by wind and rain flower nectar will
go stale flutter of despair beaten wings
muted beak took-took

HERBIPOROUS

we used to be interlinked, not bound
by economy, but living space

as a child I swallowed
pullum iecoris and cor pullum
which my grandma cut out
with care

I sucked ossium dry, the cervical
vertebrae were my favourite
I looked through the foramen
vertebrale not thinking of my own

now I sense
our alienation as assets

our market value fluctuates
from one day to the next

there is no difference between
l'homme and les oiseaux
there is a difference

I invest myself into the economy
of plantae to survive I dream
of the corpus hortus entanglement

calluna vulgaris on my forehead nephrolepis
exaltata in my shoulders kalanchoe
daigremontiana: devil's backbone is also mine
crassula ovata fingers dracaena bones
echeveria eyes geranium ears
begonia lips spathiphyllum vagina
maranta leuconeura circulation
ceropegia woodii in my chest I
loses itself deciduously

EXTINCTION ÉTUDE

Using your fingertips gather the dust
off the laptop screen showing
the photos of baiji white dolphin
and West African Black Rhinoceros.

Sprinkle the dust on your head
to get an idea of baiji white dolphin
and West African Black Rhinoceros.

You are visited by the sharp scent
of their howl, the bare sound
of their skin, their bodies skewed
shadows thrown on the wall.

Investigate the silent space and
ask if their existence started
with a drought or rain.

You sense it all as unrecognisable:
you've sensed it all before.

It shifts and changes
tiny edges of your bones:
the fracturing absence.

The echoes of their habitats are distinct
and yet within you swells the same
unutterable word.

PLANT, LANGUAGE

Breakages in the soil
unseeded vistas

the sun looks away

treeless
breathless

the wind blows
with no idea

silent hum
chlorophyllic veins

the light, at last,
through through

air particles tremble
still in wait

syncopated seeds
rooting for nothing

time doesn't count
one two no

deciduous plain
in metabolic want

multitudes
interwoven

inaudible
persistent

A BIRD IN FLIGHT

After 'A Chair in Snow' by Jane Hirshfield

A bird in flight
should be
like any other animal in motion
& in its element

yet a bird in flight is always freefluent

more than a butterfly
more than a frog or a leopard
a bird's bones are made for just one thing

the breath of the sky
and its quick changeable
shapes

not to hold marrow

not to hold time

I AM BUILDING SOMETHING

For Helena and Roshni

that is bigger than myself,
adding one part onto another.

Look, I have gradually grown a tree:
it is for you.

There are green leaves on it
and a few birds.

What tree?
A cherry tree.

What birds?
A hawk, a black bird, and a duck.

There is a goat in the shade of the tree.

Go on, take it for a walk
and have a good day.

MULTIPLICITIES OF TREES

a tree, a tree, a tree
a thought splits between them

touching the bark feels sacred and intimate

the question of the soul's eternity
comes up in a forest

it is out of place

relating to other living things
through nouns, adjectives, and verbs
is all I can do

even though my heart breaks
every single line

SOUNDING SOIL

Sounding Soil of a Nuclear Plant

Glglglglglglgl ungrungrungr rarararara dedededede glglglglglglgl ungrungrungr rarararara dedededede glglglglglglgl ungrungrungr rarararara dedededede glglglglglglgl ungrungrungr rarararara dedededede glglglglglglgl ungrungrungr rarararara dedededede

Sounding Soil of a Forest

Vwvwvwvw wuwuwuwuzzzzm mzzzmzzzmzzz zzzzzzzzuwww mlmlmluwmluwmluw zzzssszzzssszzz shshshshshsh zhzhzhz msssmssmssssmmmm mmmmssssss vtrrrrr vtreeeeee mmzzzzz sooossssooosooooosooo ffffzzzfzzzfzzzzzz nnnnaaannnnaaaanna

Sounding the Soil of the Seabed

Wawawawawawawa wowowwowo wuwuwuuwuw owowowow uwuwuwuwuw awawawawa wooowwooooowwww wuuwwuush shshhhshhh sh ssshhuuwwwww shuuwwwwwshhhh owowowsh eawoeawoea eaeaeaeaeaw weaweaweaweashhhh weashh ishhhhh

Sounding Soil of a Meadow

Grrgrrgrr grrrr tkrrrtkkkkrrr tk tkkkkkk sheeeshe grr grrrrgrrrrr shuushuuu vzzzzz vzzzzzz vzzzzzz bruuuummmzzzzzz brumzz katikitikitikitiki grrrrgrrrrruummmzzzhhhh vuuuvuuuuu wushhh thrtkrthruuuuuu gzzzzgzzzzbvgzzzzhhh vzevrtrrrrtrrrt tktktkkk

Sounding Soil of a Potato Field

- -

- -

- -

- -

SYNTHETIC LULLABY

The moon bloom imbued   into the blue
        metal islets in glow   swallow   the blue whole
further away,   fly   closer to   foam edges, the bluest   of molecules
  sound waves of   acrylic devices   receiving   over   any blue

non-linear rivers   inside you playing   slow   blues
      oh hush   the star fish is growing   its lost indigo   limb
rayon flux of a sun   washed in   cerulean air
        endless body   eased out of   the blue neoprene

oh do not fear silvery ripples in the polyester sky of blue
synthetic creatures bear arms in sea stir, azure oceanic want
hair drifts, no shaming of the cobalt flow
skin shed into the nylon echoes of a cyan harbour

unmute the rhythm of something resistant, unfinishing indigo
vinyl no longer binding bones, silence of the iris eye
ankles rotated into cloud fibre petals, no tension in the sapphire ground
collapse into unbroken sleep, the sea folded in, the bluest of dreams

THE RAIL SLEEPS IN THE SNOW

The train had been rolling for years. It came to a halt; a whistle cried. Snowdrifts grew bigger as time melted. It was advisable to choose heating over lighting, so we sat in compartments in dark silence, sucking on lollipops like there was no tomorrow. The train cafe had nothing left, apart from bottles of spirit vinegar. Our thighs relaxed into each other. By the time we arrived, it was an after-time. No announcement was made. No sound. Dust on our shoes shone like radioactive salt. Snow in our heads.

SNOW IN DEEP TIME

After Nan Shepherd

It snowed all night. I walk through a forest
deeper and deeper into its living stillness. The
evolutions of snow tell a kaleidoscopic story
of time and water. Water remembers all its
forms. The sky over a white world makes my
mind   . The crunch of boots
on the snow, how silent. Hoping to see nobody.
Noting the tracks of animals and birds. And
then suddenly, a fox dragging his brush,
followed by thin red deer, and a sounder of
wild boar. My finger finds a tunnel in the snow.

The translucent ice like fabric, crimpled and
bubbled. Crystal flutes on the bank of a pond.
A tree of glass hardening, lying low. The
electric blue of the sky hidden behind the
clouds. Some halcyon weather. A word wants
to be heard and echoed through the soft forest.
I hold it back in my throat and eat the snow.
I step onto the ice and watch the water move.
A few more seconds and it will break. I fall in.
My body, like the tree, hardening.

The stillness of the stones flung underneath the frozen stream. Still current among ice-floes and above the ice still fixation of the wind. The ghostly thin powdering of the snow. The warm sky dissolves the ice. The earth around me growing bare, brown leaves decompose. Still green grass underneath the snow. Where was I before I came here? What happened before the snow started falling?

FREEDOM AT LAST

Please don't wake me up!
I am sleeping inside a tree.

I won't answer to anyone.

A BIRD IN A TREE DOESN'T KNOW HOW TO SING LIKE A ROBOT

Golden shovel after Etel Adnan's Shifting the Silence

'Have we lost our autonomy, from conditioning to conditioning, have we become prisoners of webs, cobwebs, tightening circles that make us respond in predictable ways to the situations we face?' —Etel Adnan

Yes, these are the last few days we have
left to picnic and eat what we

haven't grown. Here's to the lost
species and spoilt soils, to our

blood's faint autonomy
flowing from

heart to brain, here's to the land's conditioning
to maintain picnic supply, and to

our conditioning
not to suppress resistance we have

to see what we
have become.

The trees are no apathetic prisoners,
they trust in the delicate delivery of

nutrients through their roots' webs.
Corporate spiders spin fractal cobwebs

of seeming happiness, tightening
its grip on our bodies dancing in circles.

Deep within us: dark and moist soil that
is readying for new seeds will make

an ancient call sound through and through us.
Even these trees in the still smoking forest will respond.

The purple mountain majesties in
the shadow of the full moon: no longer predictable.

Water from melting icebergs finds new ways
to flow into villages and towns. A myth we return to.

The manufactured sun in the
manufactured sky is beginning to crack. These situations,

repeated on loop, will be constant. And that which we,
still living, have to face.

QUESTIONING

After Anna Tsing's The Mushroom at the End of the World

I.

How to go? How to be? How to find? How to be? How to fear? How to find? How to tell? How to go? How to live? How to rail? How to put? How to seem? How to be against? How to speak? How to have? How to tell? How to look for? How to live together? How to follow? How to discuss? How to be? How to realise? How to be? How to know? How to turn out? How to know? How to propose? How to write? How to be? How to make? How to chart? How to explore? How to refuse? How to acknowledge? How to admit? How to be? How to say? How to be? How to need? How to gather? How to learn? How to be? How to force? How to pick out? How to listen? How to create?

II.

The Stone Age. The Stone Age. As I write, "anthropo-" and explore the terrain it disasters: I find myself without the than railing at those who put the moments of harmony and dissonance I was lost and empty-handed in refuses to acknowledge. Refuses to acknowledge. I'll admit it's did not know English, but it if I'm really lucky, I find and still full of promising contradictions. Of promising contradictions. Was a revelation in listening; I many species sometimes live together without I go for a walk, and however, I need something other than this: there might not be a mushrooms. Be a mushrooms. And it's not that I an unknown forest. An unknown forest. The older man everyone is going and, also, why. And, also, why. A worthwhile tale, then, I must discussing questions of classification. Questions of classification. It was tell of displacement and loss. Displacement and loss. In To live with precarity requires more am not proposing a return to simultaneous melodies and to listen for a still-bright evening when I realised spoke with have terrible stories to either harmony or conquest. Harmony or conquest. I follow handrails of stories that tell where this time of diminished expectations, I Mandarin Chinese, as did I. As did I. I was forced to pick out separate, might fear a spurt of new In order to make mushroom picking us here (although that seems useful collective happy ending. Collective happy ending. For my purposes, that practice except where I am first chart the work of this look for disturbance-based ecologies in which the term is still new – turned out he knew a little Most of the mushroom foragers I organisms as the elements that gather. Elements that gather. When I first learned polyphony, it too, and I'm not against it). Not against it). Hard for me to even say. To even say.

III.

Is it a stone? Is it age? Is it a terrain? Are these disasters? Is it a railing? Are these moments? Is it harmony? Is it dissonance? Are these contradictions? Is it a revelation? Are these species? Is it a walk? Are these mushrooms? Is it a forest? Is it a man? Is it a tale? Are these questions? Is it a classification? Is it displacement? Is it a loss? Is it precarity? Is it a return? Are these melodies? Is it an evening? Are these stories? Is it harmony? Is it a conquest? Are these handrails? Are these stories? Are these expectations? Is it a spurt? Is it a mushroom? Is it an ending? Are these purposes? Is it practice? Is it the work? Is it a disturbance? Are these ecologies? Is it the term? Are these mushroom foragers? Are these organisms? Are these elements? Is it polyphony?

I go for a walk, and if I'm really lucky, I find mushrooms. And it's not that I might fear a spurt of new disasters: I find myself without the handrails of stories that tell where everyone is going and, also, why. To live with precarity requires more than railing at those who put us here (although that seems useful too, and I'm not against it). Most of the mushroom foragers I spoke with have terrible stories to tell of displacement and loss. In this time of diminished expectations, I look for disturbance-based ecologies in which many species sometimes live together without either harmony or conquest. I follow that practice except where I am discussing questions of classification. It was a still-bright evening when I realised I was lost and empty-handed in an unknown forest. The older man did not know English, but it turned out he knew a little Mandarin Chinese, as did I. I am not proposing a return to the Stone Age. As I write, the term is still new – and still full of promising contradictions. In order to make mushroom picking a worthwhile tale, then, I must first chart the work of this "anthropo-" and explore the terrain it refuses to acknowledge. I'll admit it's hard for me to even say this: there might not be a collective happy ending. For my purposes, however, I need something other than organisms as the elements that gather. When I first learned polyphony, it was a revelation in listening; I was forced to pick out separate, simultaneous melodies and to listen for the moments of harmony and dissonance they created together.

—Randomly selected sentences from Anna Tsing's
The Mushroom at the End of the World

THE TONGUE

Some people cut it out of a cow's mouth
and place it on a plate decked with marigolds.

What does it feel like to taste a dead tongue
with yours? Is there a moment of spiritual
knowledge transmission?

The self-reflexive tongue eating itself.

So much depends on it: your voice,
your wit, your lover's satisfaction. Survival,
extinction. Your ancestors' vowels

echo in the shape of your own.
Words lost, words gained.

A cow moos in a field
of oblivious marigolds.

My tongue is made of the myriad
of linguistic cells merging without
the need for a birth certificate.

My mouth, a free zone
with no security checks nor passport
control until I step outside.

Let me speak of cow tongues
and marigolds before you take
your ruler and tell me this stanza,
just like me, is out of place.

THE CLOCK

When the oak leaf drops on a gilded cyclops
the cyclops yawns accidentally swallowing an owl

the owl remembers a churched woman
who gave birth to a chariot of stars

the stars hibernate in Cronos's pocket
which contain atoms of locust and dormice

a dormouse knows how to sleep on rising dough
to avoid falling on its face

the face of death is stuck in the hourglass
the hourglass dust covers the butterflies' wings

in the sun the wings measure my heartbeat
which goes now nownow now nownowhere

nowhere on this planet can you find a smelling clock
the smelling clock paused by a long-fingered lemur

the lemur divided crocodiles into
hours, minutes and seconds

every second I step out of the dreamtime
into the decay and delay of rooster calls

the rooster cries exhausted by
the tyranny of passing moments

momentarily insects will feast on the grandfather
whose paradox wakes me up at four in the morning

the morning folds on itself
beating its Olympic record

THE HOUSE

And for what reason are we near
gazing at the plain house
for hours? And what's the use of making vows
never to come back here

if they're broken just the next day? The open windows
painted red screech
uninvitingly, threatening the eye with broken glass. A dried plant which
stands on the rusted sill, bent in a crooked pose,

guards the emptiness of the rooms. On the porch – two hay sacks, god knows
what for. Maybe they slid down the hill on them at fever pitch
or maybe they used them as pillows. The motionless

door, left half-open, lets the echoes
of the old voices disperse into the silence. In this strange immobility each
of us wonders why the plant, the hay, the door leave us so speechless.

ALONG WITH GLASGOW

After Raymond Depardon's photographs

The rain arranges itself
on the asphalt to reflect for a moment

Steel herons crane their necks
to watch an idea propel men into anyone

People can survive a fierce weight of water
breaking from the sky or elsewhere

The symmetry of stillness and motion
the air is not yet post-industrial

Unsettled chairs litter the sky-opened
house still to be hoovered and heated

Nobody will be arriving to live
crows burst through windowpanes

Leaving rooms like kidney
stones from the fatigued body

A desolate street makes it hard to decide
which way to go, past or future

Feeling much damage feeling full
someone once loved these spaces

Not the cut price fruiterer, she'd had
enough

TIME IS MY COUNTRY, FOG IS MY LAND

After Etel Adnan

The hills
on the horizon emerge
like a foreign word, I look them up

tracing their shapes with my finger
forest paths untie into an open land,
language speaks to itself

Crossing no borders I miss
pronounce the words the way
language is owned by nobody

My words transforming into minutes,
voice does not echo in the fog,
my accent does not startle

Seconds pass yet linear time,
like the borders,
is an illusion

I catch my breath
in several languages,
no hierarchies here

I will not die
for any monolithic country
playing its anthem to the dead

Time is my country,
it counts my inhalations,
a merciless teacher untying my hair

AN IMMIGRANT'S LOVE SONG

my heart is not enough
my time is not enough
my breasts are not enough
my arms are not enough

moja rada nie wystarcza
my love is not enough
my anger is not enough
my thighs are not enough

moja twarz nie wystarcza
my fingers are not enough
my worry is not enough
my attention is not enough

moja łza nie wystarcza
my love is not enough
my curiosity is not enough
my fear is not enough

mój podziw nie wystarcza
my sadness is not enough
my hips are not enough
my mouth is not enough

mój język nie wystarcza
my eyes are not enough
my love is not enough
mój śmiech nie wystarcza

my seriousness is not enough
my playfulness is not enough
my love is not enough
mój taniec nie wystarcza

my gardening is not enough
my cruelty is not enough
my toes are not enough
moja miłość nie wystarcza

my desire is not enough
my love is not enough
my elbows are not enough
moja depresja nie wystarcza

my perseverance is not enough
my ignorance is not enough
my obsession is not enough
moja paranoja nie wystarcza

my mind is not enough
my poetry is not enough
my hope is not enough
mój akcent nie wystarcza

my writing is not enough
my love is not enough
moja miłość nie wystarcza
my love is not enough

my repetition is not enough
my love is not enough
my repetition is
my love is not

HOW TO GUIDE TO BECOMING A BRITISH CITIZEN

1 | Arrive in the United Kingdom full of hope for the future. Leave your family and close friends behind in your country of origin. They should believe you have made the right choice and encourage you. Try not to cry when you say your goodbyes as it will make it harder for your friends and family. On the plane, you can cry as much as you want.

2 | Wash your face with cold water before showing your passport. Be prepared to explain why you have come and what you are planning to do. This is your moment: tell the border control officer about your deepest dreams and aspirations, and how you are planning to contribute to the United Kingdom with your hard work and brilliant ideas. Don't worry if your English isn't perfect. You are not meant to be showing off.

3 | Stay in a hostel until you find a flat. Don't worry if you are bitten by bed bugs. Believe the receptionist when she tells you it was a mosquito.

4 | Find a small basement flat and spend almost all your money on the deposit and rent. Sign the contract. Borrow money from someone. It is a good opportunity to make friends and build connections.

5 | Contact the Home Office and pay £50 to request a form. Fill in the form. Send the form back and pay another £50. Keep all correspondence from the Home Office as it might come in useful five, ten, fifteen years later. Don't expect them to keep your documentation as they are very busy and have piles of documents to look through. It might be that they will lose your documents or shred them by mistake. Be prepared to pay every time you interact with them and do not expect them to tell you the truth or give you what you need. Be grateful even if they are hostile towards you. It is not their fault they are hostile. It is the Home Office's policy.

6 | Go to the Job Centre and register to get a National Insurance Number. Fill in a form.

7 | Open a bank account. Fill in a form.

8 | Register at the medical practice. Fill in a form.

9 | Go to the Botanical Garden. Plants have been brought here from all over the world and they managed to survive and thrive.

10 | When interacting with people in the UK, be polite no matter what. Being polite is the most important thing. If someone does or says something that makes you angry, say something polite and walk away. When alone or with a friend, you can throw things against the wall (if you're in a rented flat, you might lose your deposit).

11| Always stand at the end of any queue.

12| Print out copies of your CV and rhizome your way around the city, town, or village you have chosen to live in. Depending on the job you want, you might need to remove some qualifications from your CV.

13| Don't expect anyone to pronounce your full name. If they pronounce your first name, be grateful.

14| In winter your basement flat might be cold and damp. Wear as many layers of clothing as possible and spend time outside your flat.

15| When you get your first job, wake up with joy and enthusiasm. You will have money for rent and food!

16| Whatever your job is, keep going. One of the keys to success is adopting a native accent, but make sure you choose the correct native accent.

17| If you grew up in a socialist country, it will take you some time to understand the invisible hierarchies in the UK. Plants too are grouped into divisions and classes. Your current classification: Kingdom: United, division: foreign, class: immigrant.

18| If you have had a steady job for some time, consider moving from your basement flat into a slightly better flat, for example, on the first floor with a nice view. It is time for an upgrade! You deserve it.

19 | Having spent a few years working in pubs or temping in questionable offices, it is time to start applying for a permanent job. Yes, yes, fill in another form, but by now you're an expert.

20 | You did it! Your first permanent job. It doesn't pay well, but you have paid holiday and can rest at home when you're sick. Adopt all unwanted and neglected office plants.

21 | Enjoy your life, getting to know people and feeling at home.

22 | Oops! Brexit. Nobody expected it and now you need to decide whether to stay or go back to your country. Do not admit to stealing someone's job and taking their benefits at the same time. Every country has the right to take back control. You might not feel welcome anymore, but it is nobody's fault.

23 | If you've decided to stay, it is now time to apply for British Citizenship. It will cost only £1,800 if everything goes well. You'll need to have kept every payslip, bank statement, electricity bill, council tax bill, etc etc etc. Remember your correspondence from the Home Office? Yes, this is when you will need it. It might take you months to collect the information, but think about the reward! If you make a mistake in your application, you will have to pay the fee again.

24 | Before you submit your application, you will need to prove that you speak English (£100) and know many important things about the UK (£50). The citizenship test will cover vital information about British cricketeers, the exact dates of various battles, and the number of Henry VIII's wives. You will need to learn hardly anything about Wales, Scotland and Northern Ireland. They are less important. It's important you remember that England is a good country.

25 | When you arrive for your test, you will have your hair and ears checked for Bluetooth devices (no cheating!), you will have to roll up your sleeves and leave your belongings in a dedicated Sainsbury's bag. You will not be able to take a tissue with you (no cheating!). Don't worry about elderly people struggling to operate the outdated and user-unfriendly operating system. This is all part of the hostile environment policy! It's nobody's fault. When you leave, you will see a notice on the door 'We Hope You Have Enjoyed Your Test'. You see, the Home Office cares, even if you don't.

26 | At the citizenship ceremony, you will make an oath of allegiance or an affirmation if you don't believe in god. Wear nice clothes. You will get a welcome letter from the Home Secretary (who wouldn't want that).

27 | Congratulations, you are now a British Citizen! Do you remember how to say it in your mother tongue or your father tongue?

MY ENGLISH IS SO GOOD

A man shows me trophies from corporate wars.
I ask him who else contributed to them.
He says I might not know the words he is about to use.
I tell him I do know them.
Your English is so good, he tells me.
I switch registers, making my language dense,
I probe *what do you mean? How did it make you feel?*
He's nervous, inserting swearwords to catch a breath.
I take him by the hand, ask him to look outside:
Don't worry, I say, *your English is still good*.

I walk towards a park and see a car reverse into a fence.
A group of children runs around the grass.
The car turns on its front, down the fence and stops.
I run towards it and see a woman curled behind the steering
wheel,
I call an ambulance, keep talking to her, asking her name, her age.
Mairi tells me most accidents in Scotland are caused by foreigners.
I check her pulse, ask her if she is in pain.
I take her to the moon, show her where Poland is.
She listens to my story, she'd never heard it told
from this perspective, *Your English is so good*, she says.

The day after the Brexit vote three men approach me,
asking if I have a visa and why I am still here.
I sit them down and ask them to tell me what they know
about the 1930s, Nazi Germany, the Holocaust.
Their eloquence fades away, shrunk into three little boys
caught unprepared again for history class.
Later that day they come to say they're sorry
Your English is so good, they say, I let them listen to me
summarise how fascism starts to grow. They walk away,
shame tucked in the stitches of their suits like old dirt.

In the detention centre in Dungavel, I visit men and women,
mostly people of colour, a few white men from Eastern Europe.
I listen to a fisherman from Vietnam tell me a story
about his protest against polluted rivers in his village, the dead fish,
his time in prison, his escape, his walk through Russia
where he buried friends in snow,
being trafficked to work in Germany and England.
Your English is so good, I say, not knowing what to say.
Why are you here? he asks, *Why do you care?*
I could be here one day, I say, *the line is fine.*
Your English is good too, he says.

A LACK OF KNOWLEDGE

The deer stand in a field.
There is no question mark.

The stag's body will slowly decompose,
its soul will travel up the trees.

The wind sings its song of mourning,
the stag's body will soon be covered by moss.

My body is so fragile and full of languages.
What language will I speak to nature?

W jakim języku będę rozmawiać z naturą?

I do not know.

EMERGENCY OXYGEN

The flying fish like birds
glide in the air
aerodynamic bodies
with no scales

My body is flying inside
a Boeing 737-800 made of
aluminium, zinc, magnesium,
copper, plastic, leather

My heart is soft:
oxygen, carbon,
hydrogen, nitrogen,
calcium, phosphorus

Inside my and the fish's gut
microplastics gather like
non-compostable dust

A cup, a bottle, a carrier
bag, a fork, a plate,
a bracelet, kite string

The flying fish and I
will decompose sooner
than the plastic debris,
than the body of the plane
in the ocean

Even the emergency oxygen
falling from the panels
above our heads
won't make us last

We rise in the air
in protest
our hearts soft,
we rise in protest

PURPLE

After Paul Celan's poem 'Black'

White light
skin stuck to fake leather: the burning
teeth chatter like dice, cut rhythm

The nicotine breath of a wasp-waisted
nurse, her laughter, the hallway long
like an empty intestine

Purple light
the cough thickens in the heat,
the drip drips like seconds

The breath in and out non-stop
eyebrows stuck to the face
like always

The innermost voice towards
iris light
shines out to live

NOTES

'Female Figs Closed on All Sides, Supposed to be Monsters' was written in response to a line found in the notes to Erasmus Darwin's set of two poems *The Botanic Garden*: 'Female Figs Closed on All Sides, Supposed to be Monsters.'

'Woman Dreams of Escape' was written in response to Joan Miró's painting by the same name.

'Noonwraiths' were written in response to a Slavic myth about Południce, who, according to some sources, are spirits of young women that died a violent death either before, during, or just after their wedding. They are said to appear at noon during hot summer days, wearing torn wedding dresses causing heatstroke and even death to their victims.

'Figs Wounded with a Straw Ripen Sooner' was written in response to a line found in the notes to *The Botanic Garden:* 'Figs wounded with a straw, and pears and plumbs wounded by insects ripen sooner, and become sweeter.'

'Piekło Kobiet' translates as 'Women's Hell'.

'Synthetic Lullaby' follows the Oulipo method of Belle Absente (Beautiful Outlaw).

'Lighthouse Moods' includes photographs of a Scottish lighthouse taken by me.

'The Rail Sleeps in the Snow' was written in response to a line found in the notes to *The Botanic Garden*: 'The rail sleeps in the snow.'

'Snow in Deep Time' includes photographs of a Polish forest taken by me. It is inspired by my reading of Nan Shepherd's *The Living Mountain.*

'A Bird in a Tree Doesn't Know How to Sing Like a Robot' is a Golden Shovel of a quote from *Shifting the Silence* by Etel Adnan: 'Have we lost our autonomy, from conditioning to conditioning, have we become prisoners of webs, cobwebs, tightening circles that make us respond in predictable ways to the situations we face?'

To write 'Questioning' I've used Anna Tsing's *The Mushroom at the End of the World: On the Possibility of Life in Capitalist Ruins*, with Tsing's kind permission, as my source text. I first selected sentences from each page of the book. I then reduced the text to verbs and placed them in the same question format (part I). Part II is the initial text put through the Lazarus text mixing desk. I then selected nouns in the order they appear in the mixed text and put them in the question format (part III).

'Along with Glasgow' was written in response to Raymond Depardon's photographs of Glasgow: https://www.magnumphotos.com/arts-culture/society-arts-culture/william-boyd-raymond-depardon-1980s-glasgow/

'Time is My Country, Fog is My Land' was written in response to a line from Etel Adnan's poem 'Fog' (*Sea and Fog*): 'Time is my country, fog is my land.'

ACKNOWLEDGEMENTS

Thank you to the editors of *Footprints: Ecopoetry Anthology* (Broken Sleep Books), *Harpy Hybrid Review, Sublunary Editions, La Piccioletta Barca, Magma, Four Letter Word* (Interview Room 11), *Multiple Exposures* (Longbarrow Press), *Gutter, Blackbox Manifold, amberflora, Interpreter's House, Tentacular, -algia*, and *A Gift, Once Given, Must Not Be Spurned: The VERVE Anthology of Eco-Poetry* (Verve Poetry Press) for publishing some of the poems, or earlier versions of the poems, in this book.

'Hania at the End of the World' received special commendation and is published on the website of the Oxford Brookes International Poetry Competition.

'A Bird in Flight' was one of the winners of the Poetry Society's Members' Competition Winter 2024.

'Emergency Oxygen' was commended in the Verve Eco-Poetry Competition 2024.

My deepest gratitude to Bad Betty Press for publishing my work. To Amy Acre for her attention, care, generosity, and time in editing and designing this book. Working with Amy has been one of the most nourishing experiences of my life.

Deep appreciation to my teachers and mentors, both non-human and human. To poets, writers, and artists who have influenced my writing and helped me find my poems.

With gratitude to the Scottish Book Trust for their ongoing support and encouragement.

Thank you to my friends for your beauty, understanding, conversations, and laughing at my jokes.

My endless love to my family, in particular to my Mama and Tata, to Daniel, Kinga, and Szymon.

I dedicate this book to you all.